Lessons Learned From My Homeschool Day

Learning from the good, the bad and the icky lessons to help you through the day

Trina R. Ferguson

JAYMEDIA PUBLISHING

Copyright © 2016 by Trina R. Ferguson.

All rights reserved. No part of this book may be
used or reproduced in any manner whatsoever without
the express written permission of the publisher except for
the use of brief quotations in a book review.

Printed in the United States of America

First printing, 2016

JayMedia Publishing
9429 Nicklaus Lane
Laurel, MD 20708

ISBN 978-0-9849290-1-6

Cover photo by C L Tyson Photography, LLC

This book is dedicated to anyone on an unexpected journey in life.

God is with you and has equipped you to handle this season.

Embrace the journey and all the lessons learned.

Contents

Acknowledgments 7
Embracing the Journey: "Hello, Iced Coffee!" 9
Along for the Lessons: Meet The Family 13
Lesson　#1: The Night Before or The Morning After 15
Lesson　#2: Keeping This Cape On! 17
Lesson　#3: Say "I'm Sorry" Even If It May Not Be Enough 21
Lesson　#4: Feed Your Family First 23
Lesson　#5: Have a Plan A, B and Sometimes C 25
Lesson　#6: Stop and Listen, Even If You Don't Understand 27
Lesson　#7: Be Thankful in All Situations 29
Lesson　#8: Avoid Messjuries 33
Lesson　#9: How to Properly Handle the "I Don't Feel Like It" Blues 35
Lesson #10: Celebrate (even over the little things)! 39
Lesson #11: Face Your Fears or Your Children Will. 41
Lesson #12: Don't be "Stinky" Even Though You're Covered 45
Lesson #13: Put on Your Princess Dress (or Royal Garments) 49
Lesson #14: Study it + Focus on it + Practice it = MASTER IT! 51
Lesson #15: Do Not Soar Alone 53
Lesson #16: There is BEAUTY in the icky MESS 57
Lesson #17: My Children are Worth the Wait 61
Lesson #18: Keep Moving Forward 63
Lesson #19: Start Small 65
Lesson #20: Serve! 67
Lesson #21: Walk Away Okay 71
Lesson #22: If It Doesn't Fit, Try Again 75
Lesson #23: Don't Worry, Smile! 79
Lesson #24: No More Plagiarizing 83
Lesson #25: The Mom G.E.N.E. 85
Lesson #26: Listen & Obey (The First Time) 89
Lesson #27: Turn gloomy Into GROOOVY! 91
Lesson #28: Know the "Coach's" Voice 93
Lesson #29: Stand Up (Even If It Means You're Standing Alone) 95
Lesson #30: The Waterslide 97
Lesson #31: Back to School 101
Lesson #32: Are You Hungry Enough? 103

Acknowledgments

Thank you, God, for this opportunity to learn more than I could have ever learned about You and about myself. Thank you for not getting tired of the many confirmations that I have needed on this journey. You are truly my first love and I can't thank you enough.

Thank you, Lawrence, for encouraging me and believing that I could one day actually write a book. I am truly thankful that I have you as my husband but most importantly as my friend. I tell you often, "when I'm mad at my husband, I want to talk to my friend, Lawrence." LOL. I love you, my dear, and appreciate all that you do for our family.

To my wonderful miracles…Thank you for hanging in there with me on this journey. You have dealt with my crazy days, my fun days, my overwhelmed days, my silly days, my everything days, and you still want to talk to me and hang out with me. I love you more than you'll ever know. This journey, I will no longer call a sacrifice, but an investment – one of my greatest and biggest investments.

Many thanks to Anita, Angela, Margaret and Victoria, who were there to help me, teach me (and my children), pray with and encourage me on this homeschooling journey. I have learned so much from all of you, and I thank God that He placed you in my life. I love you and appreciate your wisdom, love, laughs and support.

To my many wonderful friends who I call family, you guys rock! Whenever I wanted to give up, you were right there with an encouraging word, a game night, a "we'll take the kids so you can have a date" blessing, a small group session (Benjamin group is the best group), a meal, or with whatever else I needed. Thank you for seeing more in me than I see in myself at times. I love you guys beyond words.

Proverbs 17:17 (New International Version) says, "A friend loves at all times and a brother is born for a time of adversity." Thank you to all of my siblings for being there during the good times, the bad times and all of the ugly times. You guys make life a lot easier and a whole lot more fun. Thank you for the bond that we all share. It's a rare thing that I truly treasure.

Last but certainly not least, to my wonderful wise mother. You "tricked" me into this journey and I love you for it! Thank you for believing that I could actually teach my children and do it well. I appreciate your loving heart, the many investments you have made in my life and for never giving up on me. I know sometimes I'm not the easiest to get along with but your unconditional love, I really do feel. I love you, mom, and thank you for being you!

Special thanks to:

C L Tyson Photography, LLC (CLTysonPhotography@gmail.com) for "capturing memorable moments" for this special project. I couldn't have chosen a better company.

My editors, Jeffrey Lyles of Lylesmoviefiles.com and Christine Johnson of JayMedia Productions, I appreciate all of your hard work!

JayMedia Productions, thank you for believing in me and publishing my first book.

Linda Tindale and family for my lovely locs and for your hospitality as you prepared me for this new season in my life. Love you all!

Embracing the Journey:

"Hello, Iced Coffee!"

Preparing to have my tonsils taken out (at 38!), I sat in the car looking over the list of all the things I could not eat or drink for at least two weeks. Then suddenly, I saw the dreaded two words – Hot Beverages. It was like the sound from horror movies filled the speakers in my car and all I could say was, "Nooooooo!!!!"

If you're anything like me, then you know two weeks without hot coffee or hot tea is like telling me to hold my breath for two weeks. I didn't care about not having food that I could actually chew for two weeks. I needed to lose weight anyway. But to tell me that I couldn't have any kind of hot beverages for at least two weeks is just plain old insane to me. I kept reading the list of can't haves and decided to reread it just in case I misread something. Well, I did. Instead of the two weeks of nothing hot to drink, it was actually four to six weeks! This was so devastating to me that I blocked the actual time frame out of my head.

I had no idea what to do. So, I decided to send my woes via text to my college buddy (and now my sister-in-law). Surely, she would understand since I have known her pretty much all of my adult life. We have had more cups of coffee and tea than one could imagine. Yes, my dear friend would totally get why I am so upset!

"…You can try Iced Coffee…" What did I just read? "…Iced Coffee?" I have no idea what she wrote before or after those awful words. I am sure it was great and sweet and wise but "you can try Iced Coffee" was not what I expected. As I sat in my car, pouting, it hit me. Iced coffee may not be a bad thing. **It's different but different doesn't always mean bad**. Right? After all, God did move me from a nice comfy job that I had grown to know and love very well, to home; and, not just to come home, but to homeschool our children. Different? Absolutely! It's definitely different especially for me. This was the equivalent of my friend's text message…"you can try Iced Coffee."

Different does not always mean that one thing is better than or worse than something else. Different, just means another option that is best for me at this point in my life. Just like the Iced Coffee. It was the best thing for me at that point because it aided in the healing process from my surgery.

It's the same when my husband and I decided to go with the plan we believed God had for our family. After many months of praying, discussing and even writing down all the pros and cons of various public schools, private schools and even homeschooling, homeschooling still wasn't our first choice. In fact, it was very close to our last choice. So, why did we decide to homeschool if it was close to our last choice?

I remember praying and asking God to make the decision clear to me. Since homeschooling was not my desire, I decided to "give" God a list of things that would make the decision clear to me. My little prayer was simply, "Lord, if this is what you want me to do, then provide all that we need to homeschool for the first year." This sounds like a nice harmful prayer but it was said with the wrong motives. I did NOT want to homeschool.

Shortly after I said "amen," my husband called to tell me that a lady was closing her daycare and was giving away a large chalkboard – For FREE! So we went to the lady's house and immediately she starts talking to me about homeschooling and how she had tons of materials for Pre-K through First Grade that she needed to get rid of. I finally gave into the conversation and shared with her the crossroad that we were currently facing. Not only did this wonderful lady give us all of her curriculum and resources, she gave us enough school supplies to last us, literally, for six years!

Even though my motive was so wrong at the time, God still covered me with His grace and mercy, and made our next steps pretty clear. It was time for us to embrace our new journey and for me to learn all that God wanted me to learn through homeschooling.

So, whether you chose to homeschool or not, I invite you to come along with me on this journey of Lessons Learned From My Homeschool Day. With each lesson in this book, you will find:

1. My Teachable Moment – As a mom, I have many stories to tell. So, why not write them down and share them with you – from my home to yours. Enjoy!

2. My Lesson Learned – Since I decided to embrace this journey, I have learned a thing or two along the way. I'm realizing that coming home may have been more for me to grow up than for my children. I'm learning through the good, the bad and the icky lessons for me and for you. Wink.

3. My Ever-Present Help – Without God, I could do nothing! So with every teachable moment and with every lesson learned, My Ever-Present Help anchors me. May the scripture(s) in this section help you in every situation you face in life.

I pray that there is something in this book that will touch you in such a way that it will change your life forever. So, sit back, relax and don't be afraid to cry or laugh right along with me. Grab a glass of iced (or hot) coffee and let's have some fun as we embrace this journey together.

Blessings!
Trina R. Ferguson

~~~~~

No eye has seen, no ear has heard, and no mind has imagined what God has prepared for those who love Him.
I Corinthians 2:9, NLT

~~~~~

Enjoy the Journey!

Along for the Lessons:

Meet The Family

Lawrence AKA SuperDad – This is my loving, caring and easygoing husband. He keeps me laughing and is the best dad in the world. Lawrence works hard to provide for our family and prays even harder as he guides our family through all of our lessons learned.

Trina AKA WonderMom – This is me! You'll find out a lot about me in this book but for now, I absolutely love watching football and movies. With all the details in my stories, one would think that I live in my own movie every day.

Christian AKA Cool C – He is our oldest and only son. This soft spoken Godly young man is full of wisdom, quick wit and energy! So, we put him in soccer. It's one of his favorite things to do to the point where he won a science fair based on soccer.

Lillian AKA Sweet Lily – Lillian is our middle child and oldest daughter. She is a nurturer and loves to take care of her loved ones (at such a young age). Lillian loves to play dress up and put together her daily outfits (down to the accessories, shoes and purse). She is also a very soft spoken child.

Caylin AKA Nugget AKA Caylin, Caylin AKA Cheekers – Caylin is our youngest child and daughter. She is full of joy, energy and very outgoing. Caylin is NOT one of our soft-spoken children. She truly keeps us laughing and on our toes at the same time. (This is one of the reasons why I have to call her name more than once sometimes.)

Lesson #1:

The Night Before or The Morning After

My Teachable Moment

It's late and I am totally exhausted from such a long day. Tomorrow is our co-op day (a day where homeschoolers come together in one location and take classes with each other). The thought of waking up early in the morning haunts my every thought. It so reminds me of my freshman college days when I made the awful mistake of scheduling classes first thing in the morning – Big Mistake! Anyway, as I sit here thinking about all the things I have to do before I even leave the house, I finally decide to learn from my mistakes.

The night before a homeschool day, happens to be the most critical part of my day. Lunches made, breakfast done (or at least thought of), bottles made, lesson plans ready and clothes laid out can be an exhausting routine especially on top of an exhausting day. **But the morning after, seems so much sweeter when you prepare the night before**. Here's what a co-op day or any homeschool day looks like without the night before preparation:

"Ahhh, Shoot!" Once again I've hit the snooze button one too many times. I jump out of bed and run through the hallway yelling "Wake up!" As I'm getting ready, I realize that I forgot to lay out the clothes for the day. Now I have to rummage through the piles of clean clothes on the floor that I never found the time to fold and put away.

During all of this, I hear Caylin and Lillian, who are 6 months and two years old at the time, chatting away and laughing. I go in to get them ready and I see Lillian trying to climb into Caylin's crib. I get Lillian down and go back to rummaging through the piles of clothes trying to find outfits for the girls now.

Finally outfits are found and the girls are dressed. We head downstairs for breakfast. One would think that it would be smooth sailing from this point on. Think again. Christian, who is now dressed and ready to go, not only has a wrinkled uniform shirt but his pants shrunk…nope, my son grew overnight again! If he wore that to co-op, I would not stop thinking that someone is probably saying "what kind of mother would let her son wear THAT!" So, of course I had to send him back upstairs to change.

In the midst of all of this, I manage to get a bottle together to feed Caylin who is now screaming. I look over at Lillian and tell her to turn on the TV. I know giving a toddler the remote control may not end well but I had to keep her busy while I made lunches. Oh she was so thrilled!

Lunches are finally made, Christian is dressed and feeding the baby and we now have 15 minutes to get to the car. "Mommy! Caylin spit up!" "Mommy, I'm huuuunnnngggggrrrrryyyy." "Mommy Caylin needs to be changed!" "Mommy, are we late again?"

A day like this does not sound fun at all. In fact, days like these, make me realize that the morning after - all the yelling, fussing, tempers flaring, forgetting things and frustrating moments - just brings about a chaotic and easily bothered mommy! Yes, even if you do prepare the night before, diapers still need to be changed and spit up actually does happen – a lot! However, when you prepare the night before, those "unexpected" happenings do not throw you off mentally, emotionally or physically as much. Take this lesson and use it in every aspect of life. Like the ant in Proverbs 6, Be Prepared!

My Lesson Learned
The Night Before is so much better than The Morning After.
Be Prepared!

My Ever-Present Help
Take a lesson from the ants, lazybones. Learn from their ways and become wise! Though they have no prince or governor or ruler to make them work, they labor hard all summer, gathering food for the winter.
Proverbs 6:6-8, NLT

Lesson #2:

Keeping This Cape On!

My Teachable Moment

Running from the building to the car, in the cold rain, while pushing a double stroller with one hand and rolling my co-op teacher bag (aka a small black suitcase) with my tote bag strapped to it, I thought I heard my SuperMom Theme Song in the background as my red cape blew with the wind.

I. AM. SUPER. MOM!

I made it to my MomMobile. The doors slide back with a push of a button and before I know it, Lillian, is in the car seat and is strapped in tight and secure. Double stroller folded up with a combination one-two and then a ttthhhrrrrreeee. Okay, so my mighty powers can't fold and put away a double stroller that easily but stay with me. I finally sit in the driver's seat, take a deep breath and smile. "Thank you, God!"

So many times I've gotten frustrated with my children for doing the same thing I do to God – not listening. My daughters believe they can do whatever their big brother does, just to wind up hurting themselves. Christian acts like he's the girls' father, only to wind up frustrated because his sisters "just won't listen!" to him. In both scenarios, I'm looking at all of them thinking to myself, "If they would just listen to me and do what they are supposed to do, then none of this would happen." So as I sit in my MomMobile, thinking about what I was just able to do, my satisfying look turns into a confused look. Am I doing too much?

As parents, we tend to wear many capes (or hats whichever works for you) **and I'm beginning to wonder if the capes we are wearing are actually draining our "super powers."** Like my children, are we trying to play a role that was not meant for us to play? Are we running around day in and day out drained because we are wearing the wrong capes? It's been awhile since I opened a comic book but I do know that "Sidekicks" know their strengths, weaknesses and who they receive their missions from – the Super Hero. The "sidekick" does not try to be the Super Hero because he/she knows their purpose. They work well together because each super hero operates in their respective roles.

I was designed to receive missions from God. He gives me the strength and the power to do the things that He asks me to do. That's it! Not the long list of things that I think would make me look good but all the things He asks me to do that makes me better! A friend of mine tends to tell me to take my cape off because she doesn't want me to be stressed.

On one hand, my friend is correct. I need to take all the "capes" off that I should not be wearing. But on the other hand, God has given me POWER and STRENGTH and MISSIONS! Keeping God first and reading the Bible, helps me to see exactly what my daily missions are to look like. Wearing the RIGHT CAPE (clothed in His Power and Strength) is actually a good thing and will help me accomplish all that He wants me to do – every difficult and not so difficult task. So from this day forward, I am Keeping This Cape On!

My Lesson Learned
Keep the Right Cape (clothed in His Power and Strength) on to accomplish what God wants you to do.

My Ever-Present Help
For I can do everything God asks me to with the help of Christ who gives me the strength and power.
Philippians 4:13, The Living Bible

Lesson #3:

Say "I'm Sorry" Even If It May Not Be Enough

My Teachable Moment

"I'm sorry" are two simple words that are packed with great meaning. "I'm sorry" are two simple words that for some reason can be the hardest thing to say. "I'm sorry" are two simple words that can be full of sarcasm and empty promises. "I'm sorry" are two simple words that we teach our children to say more often than we actually use ourselves.

Fridays are our homeschool days off/make up work days but it's not God's day off from teaching me a thing or two. I absolutely adore my lovely husband. Because of this statement, you immediately already know there's a story or a "but" that will soon follow.

I remember when Lawrence had one of his wisdom teeth removed surgically. That day, I decided to try to be the perfect nurse. I think I completely failed at this attempt when I continued to bring up the fact that I've had all four removed in the past at the same time, and I still didn't act the way that I perceived he was acting.

So my patience began wearing thin as I was currently watching a video about being kind and gentle with our husbands. The person on the video continued to talk about how we are to be kind and a helper. I heard every word, yet continued to feel the hairs on my body raise along with my internal temperature. "Trina, be kind. Trina be kind. Trina be…"

It was too late. I blurted out unkind and definitely not gentle words at a pitch I didn't even know I could reach. My husband's response brought about more of this attitude and in front of our son. Now, I am not one to "hide" the reality of marriage from our children, however, I don't want my children to ever think that in order to get your point across, you have to act like a crazy person. Everything inside of me ached from my actions and reactions.

I couldn't finish the video right away. I knew God was pushing me to form those two simple words that needed to come out of my mouth. It didn't take long to apologize to both of them but it took some time to get over the memory that my son and my husband now had in their heads.

"I'm sorry" will not take away the hurt feelings that I brought about within my husband. "I'm sorry" will not take away the example that I just sent to my son's memory that it's okay to be talked to that way or to talk to others that way. "I'm sorry" will not change the past. However, "I'm sorry" and not repeating the offense will have a better lasting effect on the one or ones you hurt.

My Lesson Learned
Say "I'm sorry" even if you feel like it's not enough to erase what was done.

My Ever-Present Help
Confess your sins to each other and pray for each other so that you may be healed. The earnest prayer of a righteous person has great power and produces wonderful results.
James 5:16, NLT

Lesson #4:

Feed Your Family First

My Teachable Moment

Every now and then, I forget that I'm not as young as I used to be. One night, I decide to pretty much pull an "all-nighter" watching a movie and just hanging with the hubby. It wasn't until 3 a.m., that I realized I have to get up in less than four hours to get ready for a very busy Sunday.

Of course I woke up late and began the mad rush to get to church on time. To help me out, Lawrence took Lillian up to the church to meet our Sister-in law for her bible study group. He then came back home to finish helping me with Caylin. Finally, we were in the car and on our way to church. "Oh my goodness, I forgot to give the kids breakfast!" I yelled, smacking myself on the forehead.

In no time, I am rushing into the church and headed to the room Lillian was in. As soon as I approach the room, I see my daughter give me this look that broke my heart. You know the look that your children give you when they receive one of their first series of shots? That look they give you right before they let out their painful cry? That look that says, "Why are you doing this to me. I trusted you." Yep, that look!

Then the dreaded words come out of a loving and caring adult's mouth, "Lillian said she's 'hungry. Did she eat breakfast this morning?" Ugh! Right in the gut. CRUSHED!

As they lovingly took care of my daughter, I walked up the stairs to set up for the youth ministry. The ladies did not judge me but, they didn't have to. I already did. "Feed your family first" I kept hearing as I set up the room for the older children to come up. "Feed your family first." It was so clear and so repetitive, that I had to stop and sit down. I kept the tears in but the guilt

I felt wasn't going away as I saw my daughter's face over and over again in my head. "Feed your family first."

After a while, I knew the words were from my loving Savior but the condemnation that set in was not. I slowly got up and reminded myself that this was a lesson that I needed to learn and one that we can all use as a reminder. "Feed Your Family First." **Sometimes we get so busy with life and others that we tend to forget to give our family the best of us**. I managed to go to the store and get snacks for the youth ministry but did not get my children anything to eat. I didn't even check to see if Lawrence was okay in the midst of all the hustle and bustle. (He's a very timely person and we were really late.) I didn't even thank him for all his help that morning.

"Feed your family first." This doesn't just mean physically. We need to give the best to our family – spiritually, physically, emotionally and mentally – instead of giving them the leftover scraps. As we seek the Lord, feeding ourselves, we should realize that all He has for us to do, He will give us the strength, the time and the ability to do it. But we must then "feed our family first" and then others second. Wives, this especially goes for us in the area of "feeding" our husband's first instead of giving them what's left of us at the end of the day (and usually we give them sleep). My wonderful wives, you know what I'm talking about! Pray and God will give you what you need to feed your husband as well.

My Lesson Learned
Remember, in all the hustle and bustle of life and the responsibilities that we know God has given to us, "FEED YOUR FAMILY FIRST!"

My Ever-Present Help
Jesus told her, "First I should feed the children – my own family..."
Mark 7:27, NLT

Lesson #5:

Have a Plan A, B and Sometimes C

My Teachable Moment

Potty training can be very trying. I've heard that girls are easier than boys to potty train, so this was music to my ears. It took Christian a very long time to want to be potty trained. I tried everything but he refused. It took my niece, who is a year younger than Christian, to tell him that only babies wore diapers. That was it! That's all it took. He never wore a diaper or training pants again.

Well, there we were years later, trying to potty train his sister, Lillian. It started off great and I was filled with much excitement. Two children (Lillian AND Caylin) in diapers can be very pricey so this was something to seriously celebrate. That milestone didn't last long, though. So, I decided to try the "underwear" method.

 Lillian was so happy to wear the potty training ones with the promise that she could wear her favorite character ones once she pee-pee'd in the potty. I even bought her a potty watch that went off every hour. We were ready and set to conquer potty training.

The first pair…wet. The second pair…wet and wet! As I sat by the school table trying to figure out what to do now, Lillian comes to me and says "Here mommy. Two pull-ups. It's not working. Here's two pull-ups." It took everything inside of me to not fall to the floor laughing hysterically. I was afraid that if she saw this emotion, then it would add to her "it's not working, let's go back to what works" mindset. Once I put the pull-up on and she walked away, I couldn't help but laugh. I am not worried because I know that one day she will be potty trained.

Lillian is not like me. I'm a planner. I tend to cross every "t" and dot every "i" twice maybe even three times. So when I am dead set on making something work, I stick to my plan even if it's not working. Sure, I have backup plans but none of them are as good as the original plan.

I don't know how many times I have pushed a curriculum to work because I have invested time and money into it. Every year, I start off with a brilliant schedule only to fall short of it midway through the year. The disappointment in my plans not working, takes such a toll on me.

I loved watching my sweet Lillian bring me the TWO options that worked before. The original plan was not working and at this point the excitement of wearing her favorite character underwear was no longer worth sitting on the potty all day and still wetting her pants. It was time to re-evaluate and move on to plan B and C. I guess she figured, if the first pull-up didn't work, then "rest assured mommy, I have one more for you." She was not disappointed at all. She moved forward and enjoyed the rest of her day.

So for now on, when I look at and browse through the boxes of new curriculum and I begin to plan out the school year, I am encouraged by Lillian that **it is okay if I have to stop and re-evaluate from time to time**. It's okay if the plans I started out with are not the plans I will end the school year with. I have not failed. I'm just moving forward to something that works so that we can all enjoy a successful school year.

My Lesson Learned
Having a Plan A, B and sometimes C is okay and needed at times in order to move forward to a plan that works and will allow peace and enjoyment for all.

My Ever-Present Help
In their hearts humans plan their course, but the Lord establishes their steps.
Proverbs 16:9, NIV

Lesson #6:

Stop and Listen, Even If You Don't Understand

My Teachable Moment

"**M**ommy, today after co-op, can we go somewhere?" Christian said as he struggled to fight back tears.

"I have a lot to do today. Why? What's up?" I responded, half listening and half paying attention to the other two children while checking my news feed on my phone.

He continued to talk as I continued to work through my to-do list. My son was really distressed and I could see that he needed to talk. Even though we had to leave the house in an hour and I had a lot more to do before we left, I stopped what I was doing, looked at him and listened. Christian began to tell me about a dream he had and how he just didn't feel right coming back home immediately after co-op. I didn't fully understand but it was clear that he was upset. We prayed, as tears fell from his eyes, for protection and wisdom in the midst of his fear.

Co-op ended and I wasn't sure exactly what to do. I decided to call Lawrence. I shared the dream with him and then added how much work I had to do when I got home. I had a plan (remember Lesson #5? You know how I am about my plans.)!

I re-evaluated the situation and decided to listen to my son. We ended up at a dear loved one's house instead of going home. The smile and relief on her face said it all – we made the right decision. She needed help – emotionally and physically.

My loved one, after many wonderful years at her job, was being let go due to budget cuts. We spent the rest of the day with her as she walked through the halls of a school she would never work at again. We made her laugh as we skated across the freshly polished floor of her classroom and danced around until people walked in to say their good-byes. As we drove her back home, instead of tears, we had precious memories to share (one which included a fight with a swarm of city mosquitoes…I'm sure I'll have a lesson learned from that one of these days.).

I still do not quite understand what Christian's dream meant, but I do know that **stopping what I was doing and listening to him, meant a world of a difference for him as well as someone very dear to us**. This lesson applies not just to your children but also to your spouse or co-worker or fiancée or sibling or friends. Stop and Listen.

My Lesson Learned
Sometimes, we just have to stop what we are doing and listen, even if we do not understand.

My Ever-Present Help
…be quick to listen, slow to speak…
James 1:19, NIV

Lesson #7:

Be Thankful in All Situations

My Teachable Moment

During one of our Bible Classes, we discussed being thankful in all situations. As my son and I went down the list of questions to figure out whether we were complainers or thankful people, the "uh-oh" expressions on our faces said it all. Sad to say, we could only answer "no" to 1 out of the 8 "do you complain when…" questions. I was determined to do better in this area.

Well, my opportunity finally came for me to apply what we learned. Lawrence has an office area in the basement and at times he works around the clock. Naturally, from time to time he gets hungry. When Lawrence is in his "work groove," he doesn't want to come upstairs to have a meal. So, he keeps a few snacks handy for these moments. Up until one very special homeschool day, this had not been a problem.

I called my husband, who went into his office that day, and I immediately began my rant. "Hello. Have you seen the peanut butter? I am so frustrated. Today has been such an awful day. We really need to go grocery shopping. I don't have it in me to go today. Nothing is working out! Then I went to make lunch and we don't have anything that matches. I know we had peanut butter and I was going to make peanut butter and jelly…"

"Oh, it's downstairs," my husband calmly interrupts my rant.

"WHY IN THE WORLD IS PEANUT BUTTER DOWNSTAIRS!" I said.

"I needed a snack," he says with a smile on his face.

How do I know he had a smile on his face? I took a training course during our dating/engagement season when we would spend countless hours on the phone. Joking. Seriously, wives can tell when their husbands are smiling on the phone.

Lawrence did apologize but my irritation would not go away. I wasn't finished expressing how upset I was that the peanut butter was not in the kitchen. As I continued, I turned to face the pantry where I saw a lot of food sitting there. I immediately stopped and said "Thank you Lord that I even have peanut butter to eat" followed by a heartfelt apology to my husband.

At that moment, I began to think of all the people in the world who don't have food in their cabinets. I was actually complaining about 1) mismatched food (Really?!?!?! Who does that?) and 2) the inconvenience of having to go downstairs to get peanut butter, when there are so many people who would love to have those options.

This was something so trivial to complain about but how many times have I complained in the last 24 hours? 12 hours? 2 hours? In the last 30 minutes? It's really sad how often we complain about things. What's even worse, hearing our children take on our complaining attitudes.

I don't know how many times I get upset with my children for having an attitude when they do not get their own way or when I "inconvenience" them during play time or TV time to help me with something. Isn't that how we treat God when we are "inconvenienced" by someone or something He sends our way on a busy day?

We complain about how much we have to do at home, at church, for our family, for other people…complain, complain, whine, whine, whine, whine, whine! That's us! We tell our children to stop whining or to fix their faces when they are upset or disappointed. We tell them to change their attitudes and to be thankful when they cannot have what they want. **Believe it or not, but our children are only imitating what they see and what they hear from us (not just from other children)**.

We have a "Thankful Wall" in our kitchen. This wall is full of pictures of things that we are thankful for, things that God has done in our lives. Every Memorial Day, we take the pictures down and begin new thankful pictures. When we have a complaining or any negative attitude, one family member takes that "troubled" family member to the Thankful Wall until the attitude changes. Do you or your family members struggle with this issue? Find a special way that will remind your family to stop complaining and start thanking!

My Lesson Learned
Be thankful in all situations and you will see a change in you and in your children.

My Ever-Present Help
Do everything without complaining or arguing.
Philippians 2:14, NIV
Be thankful in all circumstances, for this is God's will for you who belong to Christ Jesus.
1 Thessalonians 5:18, NIV

Lesson #8:

Avoid Messjuries

My Teachable Moment

"**M**OOOOMMMMMYYYY!!!" I playfully ran from the kitchen, pretending to rescue Christian from a spitting up baby. Before I knew it, I was on the floor screaming in pain. Another messjury...sprained ankle and bruised foot. Earlier that week, Lillian turned to go down the hallway, tripped on something and hit her chin on a linen chest...another messjury.

Just in case you haven't picked up on the definition of a messjury, it is an injury that is the result of a mess. You see, as I was running, I totally did not see Lillian's play broom right in the middle of the floor. As my daughter was going down the hallway, she totally did not see the clothes in front of the washer or the corner of the chest that was now sticking out from the wall. So many times, my family has suffered messjuries because things are not put away properly.

Now, I'm not saying that your house has to be perfect but it needs to be organized enough to keep messjuries from happening. Kids are going to get hurt from time to time and if you are as clumsy as I am, then you too will get hurt from time to time inside the house. Those injuries are going to happen whether your house is in order or not. **Messjuries, though, can be avoided if everyone takes the time to put things away immediately after using them**.

As I was sitting in urgent care, I began to realize that messjuries do not just affect you physically. It affects a person or family emotionally, mentally and even financially. Let's take a look at how:

Physical Messjury: an injury caused by a messy home, room or space

Emotional Messjury: a negative mood as a result of a messy home, room or space. Some people have been known to not sleep well when their bedroom is a mess. It can also be the mood you feel when your mom or mother-in-law comes over and ask you if you need help cleaning…Ouch!

Mental Messjury: a state of being or feeling confused because of the chaotic mess you have around you. Some have been known to walk into a room and forget what they went in there for because the mess overloaded their brain. (I do believe this is what happens to me a lot and it has absolutely nothing to do with age!)

Financial Messjury: paying additional co-pays and/or purchasing an item that you already have but cannot find. These messjuries can sneak up and before you know it, you're hit big time financially.

I know we are all tired and very busy. However, taking a few minutes to straighten up or put things back after you use them, will save you from the effects of a messjury.

My Lesson Learned
Messjuries take up more time and cost more than you taking a little bit of time to straighten up or put things back after you use them.

My Ever-Present Help
*If anyone, then, knows the good they ought to do and doesn't do it,
it is sin for them.
James 4:17, NIV*

Lesson #9:

How to Properly Handle the "I Don't Feel Like It" Blues

My Teachable Moment

I woke up early in the morning not wanting to do anything. Absolutely nothing! I knew right away this was going to be a day full of the "I don't feel like it" blues. As I lay in bed, I began to think of all the times Christian didn't feel like doing school work or team responsibilities (aka chores) or anything else that did not deal with a video game, a movie or toys. It works my nerves when I have to see the attitude after I ask him to do something followed by "I just really didn't want to do _____."

Since I'm trying to be the responsible one here, I decided to fight this "I don't feel like it" blues and teach my children how to handle this emotion properly. Within 5 minutes of realizing this, the two oldest begin fussing over the space in the bed...MY BED, MY KING SIZE BED! They are both tiny little things and they are fighting over space that happens to be MY space! Right then and there, the "I don't feel like dealing with this stuff today" blues came roaring out like a lion. Failed!

We head downstairs and it was one "I don't feel like it" after the next and they were all coming from, you guessed it, me! I finally sat down at the school table and calmly told Christian how I felt. I told him that this was one of those days that I just didn't have it in me and honestly I don't feel like having it in me. Christian's response put me to shame! Shame, I tell ya, SHAME!

"Mommy, I know how you feel. Last Friday when you weren't here, I went downstairs to play my video games. Daddy didn't feel right about it and told me to read a chapter or two in my book and then tell him about it. At first, I was upset and then I thought to myself, 'this actually is a good thing.

This will help me with my education and I probably do need it.' So I read my book without an attitude." This is coming from a child who we have struggled with for at least the past 3 years just about every single day with his attitude. All I could do was smile.

All the things that had taken place earlier that day, could have been for my good. Funny, this month our scripture memory is Romans 8:28 (NLT), "And we know that God causes everything to work together for the good of those who love God and are called according to His purpose for them."

As the day went on, things didn't get better at all. In fact, they got worse. I tried everything to get out of this funk. I read scriptures, I listened to the children sing songs to entertain Caylin, I prayed, I kept moving forward but things just kept happening.

Lillian's Plan B (earlier chapter…aka her pull-up) failed! She blessed my kitchen floor in a not so nice and not so clear kind of way. Thank you strawberries, grapes and apple juice! Knowing the kind of day that I already had, my son says "Mommy, don't worry about it. I'll get it." Such sacrifice (Christian hates anything that stinks except himself) and such compassion he had throughout the day. Of course, I did not let him do that for me, but his willingness and his understanding taught me a few lessons on how to properly handle the "I don't feel like it" blues.

First, talk about it instead of allowing everyone to guess what's going on with you. Second, understand that all of what you are going through and feeling, God will work out for good (it will benefit you and others). Third, be compassionate the next time your child has the "I don't feel like it" blues.

My day did not stop because I didn't feel like doing anything. The same goes for our children. They still have to do what we ask them to do but show more compassion and understanding since we all at one point or another, deal with the "I don't feel like it" blues!

My Lesson Learned

*Your day may not get any better and the "I don't feel like it blues" may linger around but focus on the bigger picture – God is still working it out for your benefit as well as for others.
So, look up and keep moving forward.*

My Ever-Present Help

*And we know that God causes everything to work together for the good of those who love God and are called according to His purpose for them.
Romans 8:28, NLT*

Lesson #10:

Celebrate (even over the little things)!

My Teachable Moment

I'm sitting at the kitchen table, when out of the corner of my eye, I see Christian coming into the kitchen. He stops right beside me and breaks out into this two-step, slide and then this crazy dance! I couldn't help but give him the head-to-the-side look that says "o-kay." With the biggest smile on his face, Christian shouts out "I took the paper out of my workbook without ripping it!" Then breaks out into, what I like to call, the Happy Geek Dance.

The Happy Geek Dance is only done when you are so filled with excitement that every ounce of rhythm that may be in your body, cannot catch up to the excitement that is bursting through your limbs. This dance is only done at home. I repeat. This dance is ONLY done at home!

Well, until now. I accidentally showed a dear friend of mine (and one of my editors), Jeff, The Happy Geek Dance. He told me that after almost 20 years, God blessed him with a long awaited gift. I couldn't control it. My mind said "hold it in" but before my brain was able to send that message to my body, it was TOO late. It came out in such a way that he said "ohhhh, that's the Happy Geek Dance." Oh my goodness! Did I really just do that in public? And at church (of all places)! Since that accident took place, I have tried to keep The Happy Geek Dance hidden.

However, after seeing Christian break out into his own version of The Happy Geek Dance, I decided to break out my dance more often. **We have to celebrate life – the big and the not so big victories**. Being able to tear a page out of his math notebook was huge for Christian. He had been practicing this skill for the past two years and was finally able to achieve his goal.

Why not celebrate over a workbook page you didn't rip this time? Why not celebrate over the load of laundry you were able to get done today? Why not celebrate over getting from Point A to Point B in your car without road rage stirring up on the inside (or the outside)? Why not celebrate you were able to take a shower before noon or actually wash your hair and style it while the baby is sleeping? Why not celebrate when you are able to have dinner on the table and it's not processed or fast foods? Why not celebrate?

As a homeschool mom, I do not get the accolades that I received when I worked outside the home. I don't get the "Outstanding" evaluations along with a monetary bonus. I don't get to close my office door to take a breather before my next task. But what I do get is to be able to stop what I'm doing and celebrate over the little things with my children. So whether you work outside the home or not, whether you receive the accolades or the bonuses or the quiet time without little fingers poking out from under the door or not, don't forget to celebrate.

My Lesson Learned
Celebrate (even over the little things)!

My Ever-Present Help
"Rejoice always..."
I Thessalonians 5:16, NIV

Lesson #11:

Face Your Fears or Your Children Will…

My Teachable Moment

It wasn't a coincidence that on three different occasions in one day, I was told to face my fears or they will appear in the lives of my children. I know that "God has not given us the spirit of fear… (2 Timothy 1:7)" however, I have to admit, I do have a lot of fears. I've never been a risk taker at all. In fact, growing up, the first day of school was one of my greatest fears. I acted like meeting new people was a risk I wasn't quite willing to take. It's crazy because I've never considered myself to be a shy person at all. However, the thought of meeting new people, scares the mess out of me. What if they don't like me? What if they think I'm weird? What if they find out where I'm from? What if?

Unfortunately, these fears have grabbed hold of me so much as an adult, that I see them playing out in my children. They are similar to me when it comes to new people, small crowds, large crowds…we don't tend to say much at first. It's actually worse in my children. I'll at least mask my fear, but them, it's written all over their faces and in their body language. My fears, since I was a little girl, are now showing up in the lives of my children but in a deeper way. It's like the grip of fear squeezes tighter and tighter with every generation.

We've lived in our current neighborhood before Christian was even born. Unfortunately, since he was able to go outside and play, not one time has he played with the neighborhood kids (except for my neighbors' children who are 4 and 7 years younger than he is). It wasn't because I told him not to either. It was fear. The same fear that I dealt with growing up and still face now. Why was he afraid to meet them or play with them? They've never shown us any reason to be cautious of them? So where is this fear coming from? Yup, me!

After a summer of negative comments from him about the amount of children now in our neighborhood, I finally asked Christian if he wanted to play with the kids. His response, "if they ask me then I will." Now this solidified my theory on where he got his fear from. I don't like taking the risk of asking because I am afraid the answer will be no. Christian is just like this, therefore, we wait. We wait until someone shows interest in us. We wait until someone asks.

The response "If they ask me, I will" continued to play over and over again in my head until I finally got out of the car, walked up to one of the mothers and began asking questions about her sons (and the other kids). Filled with anxiety, sweaty palms and all, I knew I had to do this for my son. Christian had to see my response. I had to break this cycle. The mother introduced the kids to Christian and off they went playing football in front of our house.

I went inside and FREAKED OUT! LOL I had no idea how to handle this but I knew it had to be done. To help me calm down, Lawrence went outside to play with the kids. I went upstairs, opened the windows, walked away from them and prayed. I prayed for peace, safety and wisdom. My husband and I still were cautious, which is not a bad thing; however, I was able to acknowledge that my children are in God's hands.

While I was praying, I also had to realize that maybe the fear of the neighborhood kids impacting Christian negatively, could actually turn into him being able to practice what is taught at home...Love and being a Godly example. I also had to realize that maybe they weren't the problem at all. The problem, lies within me and all of my "what if's".

When Christian came in from playing with the children so that he could get ready for soccer practice, he had such a pep in his step and a huge smile on his face to match. He truly enjoyed himself, and wanted to play with the kids again (and he did and continues to do so). Now, I have to work on all the other fears that I see rising up in both Christian and Lillian. The baby, Caylin, she shows NO FEAR of anything! Lord, help us!

We all have fears, some are very valid and you do need to have a healthy fear when dealing with certain things. However, understand that if you don't face those unhealthy fears, your children will have to face them and it will be tougher on them than it has been on you. Someone recently told me, that **my fears will keep me and my children from experiencing so much in life**. I don't want to be the reason why they cannot enjoy the things God has given to us…nature (yucky), animals (stay away), new relationships (scary)…Our children have their own fears and they don't need us to add to them.

My Lesson Learned
*Facing your fears is the hardest part, but once you do,
it will leave you so fulfilled and at peace.*

My Ever-Present Help
*Trust in the Lord with all your heart; do not depend on your own
understanding. Seek His will in all you do,
and he will show you which path to take.
Proverbs 3:5-6, NLT*

Lesson #12:

Don't be "Stinky" Even Though You're Covered

My Teachable Moment

Some lessons that I have had to learn, came from very messy and icky situations. With that said, folks, this is a lesson learned from an icky homeschool day. You've been warned! Proceed at your own risk.

On this particular morning, Caylin blessed us tremendously with a nice diaper surprise. My day time diaper team was in full effect.

"Christian, get the bag. Lillian get the wipes and a diaper for your sister. Caylin, really? Right now?"

Within less than a minute, all that I needed for this icky mission was right at my fingertips. Christian holds the bag for me as I use wipe after wipe after wipe, after wipe…you get the picture. Finally, Caylin was nice and clean.

I proceeded to ask my son to pick up a wipe that was sitting on the floor. It was from Caylin spitting up (oh I didn't mention all the bodily functions that were going on at this time…yeah, icky!). At this point, I assumed Christian did not hear me because I had to ask him again to pick up the wipe for me. His hesitation made me think he thought it was from the icky battle we just fought. I had to stress to him that the wipe was okay; I just needed him to put it in the bag he was currently holding.

Christian's confused look, followed by him moving the dirty diaper bag up and down, made me ask him what was wrong.

"I don't want to get the stinky diaper on the floor," he responded.

"It's okay," I said, "It's covered by the bag."

Immediately I thought about all the "stinky" stuff (sin) that's in me and how I am covered by the blood of Christ. My exact thought was "it's ok. I'm covered by the blood." Now this isn't to say that my sin is okay or that anyone else's sin is ok. But it was a reminder that 1) God's not finished with us yet and 2) because **we are covered by the blood, we should strive to do better**.

I love how Christian, even after I told him that the diaper would not get on the floor because it was covered by the bag, was still very careful with the bag. He didn't just say "okay" and drop the bag on the floor and walk away. He carefully held the stinky bag higher so that he could bend down to get the wipe. He didn't rush it but didn't take his time either.

What a cool way to think about sin (well at least I thought it was cool)! Those who have trusted and believed that Jesus died on the cross for our sins and that He rose again and is now in Heaven with our Heavenly Father, are covered! His death on the cross and resurrection allows us to be forgiven and our sins wiped away. However, even though we are covered and our sins are washed away, we should still raise our sin up to God (confessing them to Him) and carefully handle the tasks God has set before us: 1) telling others about His love and forgiveness ("Go and make disciples…" Matthew 28:19) and 2) showing love towards others ("love your neighbor as yourself" Matthew 22:39).

Sometimes, in the busyness and frustrations of life, we tend to "dump" our "stinkiness" onto others, not stopping to care about how much we may be messing them up. Christian was so cautious about not messing up our carpet – something so insignificant that can be cleaned up pretty easily with our carpet steamer. If only, we as believers (Christians) could be so cautious and so caring about others.

My Lesson Learned
No matter what icky mess or mood you are in; don't be stinky even though you are covered!

My Ever-Present Help
"...For the accuser of our brothers and sisters has been thrown down to earth—the one who accuses them before our God day and night. And they have defeated him by the blood of the Lamb and by their testimony.
Revelation 12:10-11, NIV

Lesson #13:

Put on Your Princess Dress (or Royal Garments)

My Teachable Moment

My girls absolutely love princesses. They dance around in their princess dresses; and, at times you will even hear them announce to everyone that they are princesses. I love it! We remind them often that they are God's special princesses. So, I was baffled by a conversation that I had, one day, with Lillian.

"Mommy."

"Yes, sweetheart?"

"I need my princess dress."

"You already have one on."

"No, mommy. This one is dirty. I need another one from upstairs."

"You have another one right there," I said as I looked in her dress up bin.

"No, mommy. I want to be a princess. I need my princess dress. I want to dance."

Immediately, my heart sank. My daughter, at age 2, believed that she needed to wear a "princess" dress in order to be a princess.

I looked at her and simply said, **"honey, you're already a princess, even when you wear pants."** The look on her face was priceless! Of course, Lillian didn't believe me. So, she went upstairs to find another dress. My "you're a princess just the way you are" speech didn't change a thing that day. But it did get my mind going!

The girls like to wear their dresses, not just to dance or be a princess, but they wear them for their daddy (and mommy and brother at times). Whenever they put one on, one of them starts the, "Daddy, look at me," chorus. They want Daddy to see how pretty they look in their princess dresses.

We too have Princess Dresses (or Royal Garments). "Therefore, as God's chosen people, holy and dearly loved, **clothe yourselves with compassion, kindness, humility, gentleness and patience**" (Colossians 3:12, NIV). You are already royalty when you become a member of God's family. Just like my daughters are already our princesses. I like to remind my children that when they leave our house, they are representing our family. It's the same principle with God's family. We are to put on our royal garments every day to show others His beauty, His love, His compassion, His kindness, His royal status!

My Lesson Learned
Before you leave your house, remember to put on your Princess Dress (or your Royal Garments)!

My Ever-Present Help
Therefore, as God's chosen people, holy and dearly loved, clothe yourselves with compassion, kindness, humility, gentleness and patience.
Colossians 3:12, NIV

Lesson #14:

Study it + Focus on it + Practice it = MASTER IT!

My Teachable Moment

In a typical school day, we cover many subjects and topics - some very fascinating and some not so much. It seems like Christian really enjoys homeschooling and the majority of the things we do. So it baffles me, when people ask Christian what is he learning or doing in school, his response is "ummmm" and then turns to look at me as to say "do you remember what we learned?" Really, son! All the hard work and care I put into personalizing these lessons for him and he doesn't remember what we learned. I can't tell you how frustrated I have gotten in the past about this very scenario.

Then one day someone told me, "He doesn't know because he truly didn't learn it." "Blah to you," is what I really wanted to say (I know very mature). But as I tucked away my hurt feelings and really took the time to get over myself, I had to listen to the wisdom of a veteran homeschooler. She was actually right.

Christian can tell you about every scenario possible in a video game. Why? Because he has studied it, focused on every aspect of it and practiced it over and over again until he mastered it. When Christian takes a math test, the parts he answers correctly, sometimes has taken him weeks or even months to conquer. However, once Christian masters the concept, it becomes so easy to him and he usually does not forget it.

Sometimes as homeschool parents, we want to get through the text book to feel like we have accomplished our school year goal. However, as I have yet to finish a non-math book, I am learning to relax a bit. I would much rather Christian master a few things than to not know much of anything we learned.

I have realized the same thing about God's Word. *I would much rather master a few scriptures and lessons from the Bible, than to be able to quote a lot of scriptures with no evidence what so ever that I am practicing what I am quoting.*

Now, I am not saying to not try to complete your textbooks or to just master a few scriptures in your life and keep on moving. No, I am saying that sometimes small chunks at a time are better than a boatload of information. Sometimes I receive wonderful revelations from reading the Bible but by the end of the day, I can't remember what I read or learned during my morning Bible time. It frustrates me because I so want to remember what God reveals to me.

There are so many wonderful revelations and so many wonderful lessons. How can I possibly remember them all? By doing what Christian does when he is determined to "conquer" something. I will study that scripture or passage, focus on every part of it (by writing it down) and then practice it (apply it) over and over again in my life, until I have mastered it. It may take me more than a year to read the bible or a book in the bible or even a chapter in a bible, but, I will master what God reveals to me (instead of moving on just to say I read something in the Bible).

My Lesson Learned

Don't move on until you've mastered what you are trying to learn. (And don't feel bad about the length of time it may take you.)

My Ever-Present Help

Let perseverance finish its work so that you may be mature and complete, not lacking anything.
James 1:4, NIV

Lesson #15:

Do Not Soar Alone

My Teachable Moment

This lesson started when Christian dropped Caylin. He felt awful! As Christian was checking on her, I asked him to step back so I could see if Caylin was okay. Instead of just stepping back, Christian ran downstairs away from the incident. I knew immediately what was going on with him. So once I calmed Caylin down, I called Christian back upstairs, where we were sitting.

My son has a tendency to "run" and isolate himself when he gets in trouble or when he feels like he has "messed up." I used to allow this because sometimes Christian just needed time to regroup. Then that dreadful day happened when he said to me that he's constantly hurting people and doesn't understand why he's still here. So when Christian ran away from the situation, I knew where he was going and what he was thinking.

Later on that day, I watched a special about Eagles (the bird not the football team). Fascinating, I might add, but Lillian, at age two, thought it was "disgusting" and asked if we could watch something else. Now, she enjoys nature shows and sharks! (This is funny because one of my many fears… Sharks!)

Anyway, in the documentary, they showed a female eagle who had a fish in her claws. She was taking it back to her babies when out of the blue, another eagle comes, attacks her and tries to take the fish from her. The mother eagle must have known that the intruder wasn't just after the fish; because, earlier the eagle had been eyeing her babies. The mom eagle was not just protecting dinner, she was protecting her babies and her home. They fought until the mom eagle let go of the fish.

Now, here's where it gets interesting. The mom eagle goes and gets help from the "dad." I like to call him her husband (what can I say, I'm a hopeless romantic). Her husband in an instant heads out and grabs the fish from the eagle, who thought it had won this battle. Ha, not yet buddy!

Well, the dad and the intruder both fly into trees as they continue the fight for the fish until the intruder finally gives up. The dad flies out of the trees, meets up with his wife and they soar together, as they take their victory lap around the sky, circling their babies at the same time. It was absolutely beautiful!

Just like the eagle who became an enemy to the family trying to take something from them, we too have an enemy. This enemy is trying to take something from us – life…life from our children, life from our homes, life from our marriages…our lives!

When I told Christian to come back upstairs that day, we sat and chatted. I let him know that one of the worst things to do is to run and hide. **The enemy so wants us to be isolated. He doesn't want us to take that victory lap especially while soaring with someone else.**

I've told Christian in the past, what his name means (a follower of Christ), and that God was not finished with his assignment here on earth yet. I explained to my son that the next time the enemy wants to take something from him, stand up tall and remind yourself of your name. Let the enemy, and anyone else who comes along, know that God is not finished with you yet and that you have a purpose that doesn't involve them.

On this day, I just needed to remind Christian that we are all in this (life) together. There will be times that we mess up and there will be times where we will beat ourselves up because of it. However, do not isolate yourself.

Just like the eagle, we all need someone to help us "soar" through those tough times; you know, those times when we feel like we have nothing left. There will also be times where we need our time to regroup; however, in those times, take those regroup moments when you are not completely tapped out.

When you're tapped out, that's when the enemy comes right on in and tries to take life from you. Instead, tap into your spouse or a trusted friend. Someone who can and will lead you back to Christ (our Ever-Present Help). Someone who will remind you of who you are and who you belong to! Whatever you choose to do, please do not soar alone! The eagle that soared alone, ended up in the trees (literally) with absolutely nothing.

My Lesson Learned
Soaring through life alone, may lead to an empty and unfulfilling life. It's pretty dangerous too.

My Ever-Present Help
As iron sharpens iron, so a friend sharpens a friend.
Proverbs 27:17, NLT

Lesson #16:

There is BEAUTY in the icky MESS

My Teachable Moment

Caylin, at 8-months old was moving - quickly I might add – and getting into everything! If you have ever had a little one in your house, then you know what that means. It's time to get on the floor and move around as you spot the little things they may spot and put into their mouths. Unfortunately, some of us, by the third child, may not do this proactive thorough inspection. Instead, we vacuum in hopes that we were able to pick up everything our little movers will spot. Then we run shouting, "noooo!" as we try to stop them from putting something into their mouths.

Well, on this day, after cleaning (very well) and vacuuming, I was very surprised to hear Caylin choking as I was in the middle of teaching the other two children. After all, what could she be choking on? Without hesitation, of course, I ran, picked her up and scooped my finger through her mouth. It wasn't easy because my joyful healthy baby girl loves to eat, smile and keep things from you (Caylin treats this as a game).

I had no idea what was in her mouth. Surprisingly, I was very calm yet actively pursuing this thing that Caylin seemed to be choking on. I went in one more time trying to scoop whatever it was out without causing her to go into a panic.

"Lord, help me."

Within seconds of me saying this, out came her lunch all over my cute black outfit I was able to put together just before my husband left for work. (Side note: some of you know how important the clothing detail is. It was an actual outfit and not the usual yoga pants and t-shirt my husband sees me in.)

Okay, back to the story. Caylin is choking and now I'm covered in her regurgitated lunch. Down it went, inside and outside my shirt, down my pant leg, onto my shoes and finally on the exercise mat we just put down for Lillian to practice her tumbling skills.

With my older two looking how I felt, they simultaneously said, "ewwww, that's disgusting," while Caylin smiled and tried to grab hold of the mess that just came out of her.

I went searching for whatever it was that she was choking on. Nothing!

As I wiped up the last bit praying that whatever it was doesn't hurt her and that it comes out at some point, Caylin (still sitting right next to me) coughed and out came bottle #1 (breakfast)! Immediately, I had to scoop her up because she grabbed something and tried to put it back into her mouth. Did I mention that some of my lessons learned were pretty icky?!? Sorry.

As I searched through this icky mess, I finally spotted a long and wide piece of clear plastic! I still don't know where it came from, but the lesson that hit me right away was "Just wait. There is beauty in the mess. Don't miss it." The plastic, that was the cause of the mess, wasn't beautiful at all; but, the fact that my daughter was no longer choking and that she was okay was beautiful.

Whatever you may be going through right now may not be pretty or beautiful at all. The cause of the icky mess is awful, ugly, horrible, unfair…But the end result, the stuff that comes as a result of the icky mess, that stuff is beautiful. Sometimes, I get caught up in trying to figure out what's causing the icky mess that I overlook the process and the beautiful end result.

That day, instead of continuing to search through the icky mess for something that was not there at first, I began to clean and pray. The icky mess could not remain on my floor. That would just be gross.

The icky mess in your life cannot just remain in your life. You have to clean it up! How do you do that? With every wipe, I prayed. So with every tear, pray for those involved in the situation. With every question, take it to God. With every down mood, hug your children or your husband or a loved one. With every doubt, wipe it away with a thankful picture or a thankful list.

This icky mess will not remain in my life and I pray that it doesn't remain in yours. I am on a mission to get it cleaned up! I don't know exactly what's causing the icky mess but it will eventually come out. However, ***I'm no longer looking for what's causing the icky mess. I am now looking for the beautiful end result. I don't want to miss it***.

My Lesson Learned
*God makes everything beautiful in His time. Stay focused on Him through prayer and reading the Bible.
Then look for the beautiful end result!*

My Ever-Present Help
*So let's not get tired of doing what is good. At just the right time we will reap a harvest of blessing if we don't give up.
Galatians 6:9, NLT*

Lesson #17:

My Children are Worth the Wait

My Teachable Moment

I really think I'm addicted to my cell phone. There, I said it! It's pretty sad when you're sitting at a red light and you begin to fidget because you are bored. Since the hands-free law was passed in my state, I've made a conscious effort to not even look down when my phone beeps letting me know I have a text message waiting. This had been pretty easy until…

I had been waiting for a while to receive a particular text message and it finally came. I immediately picked up my cell phone without thinking and began to read it and respond. I was in the car, driving with my children in the back. Suddenly I heard, "your children are worth the wait."

I can't believe how selfish and irresponsible I was in that moment. I put the cell phone down. However, on the inside I kept thinking about the text message and how I needed to get to my destination quickly so that I could finish my response before I forgot about it.

"Your children are worth the wait." Again, this sentence rang loudly in my ears. I finally slowed down and began to enjoy the ride with my children. We arrived at our destination safely and stress-free.

For the remainder of the day, I could not get that sentence out of my head. It started with not texting or even picking up the phone while driving because my children's lives are worth waiting to respond to a text message or phone call. Then it went to other areas of my life.

Some days, I spend so much time cleaning and organizing that by the end of the night, I feel like my children did not enjoy their day and neither did I. Now, I'm not saying don't clean (remember, "Avoid Messjuries"); however, I am saying that children grow up quickly and soon we will not have the opportunity to play with them, read to them or even dance with them. The house can wait. Their lives can't!

There are many things that I desire and most of them, cost money…lots of it too. Living on one income has not been the easiest journey. Many of my desires, over the years, have been put on hold. I really wish I were the kind of mom who is so content with what she has and doesn't even think about the sacrifices being made. I am working on it though, just not there quite yet.

However, even in this area, I'm realizing that my children are worth the wait. Spending this time with them, teaching them, will only last for a quick season. Their lives are worth me waiting for the things I desire. Extra sleep - my children climbing in bed with me, feet in my face and all - their closeness is worth me waiting for a moment to get an extra few hours of sleep.

Life is too short. Life with your children in your house is even shorter. So, **put down the phone, leave that pile of laundry there for another day, maybe not work that extra hour today** (if you don't have to) **and show your children that they are worth the wait!**

My Lesson Learned
Show your children that they are worth the wait.

My Ever-Present Help
Children are a gift from the Lord…
Psalm 127:3, NLT

Lesson #18:

Keep Moving Forward

My Teachable Moment

Listening to Christian read for the first time has to be my favorite moment in my homeschooling journey. It happens to be my favorite because, I remember the tears, the struggles, the speech issues, and the times I questioned whether or not I was the right person to teach him. Every now and then I still stop and smile thinking to myself, "Wow! He's reading! Thank you, Lord, for using me."

Well, on this day, I had one of those moments but it had nothing at all to do with listening to my son read. Sometimes as moms, we have a tendency to take care of everyone but ourselves. Then one day we look up and with tears in our eyes we say, "What happened? What did I do to myself?"

I decided that my family needed me to be healthy. So, I made appointments for myself that I haven't made in years (and this is so not an understatement). One appointment after the next was a reminder that I have spent years of neglecting myself. I hit my all-time health low, which sent me to my mom in tears and true anguish. "Why did I do this to myself?"

As my mom wiped my tears through the phone (moms can do that, you know…at least super moms like mine), she reassured me that things were going to be okay. I don't know if my family is anything like yours but word travels FAST in my family. The thing I love about them, even if they didn't hear about what was going on, they must have sensed something because I received 3 calls from 3 out of 5 siblings (and only one knew about what was going on). Without talking about anything, my other two siblings made me smile either through Facebook or a quick "here talk to your niece" who gave me some of the best news I've heard this year. God knows what we need and when we need it.

So, in the "presence" of my mom and my siblings, I was reminded of that very special moment when I heard Christian read for the first time. **The journey was hard and many tears fell but he kept moving forward.** Christian didn't focus on all the times he messed up on a word or the times his speech issues caused him to say a word differently than his peers. He didn't focus on the days when he would cry because it was too hard or when he would see me cry because it was too hard. Nope, my son focused on the achievement!

Christian didn't take time out to focus on all the tough times during the school day or the tough speech therapy sessions. He spent his time smiling at the fact that he could read. Years later, Christian doesn't stop in the middle of a book and dissect how he messed up in the past or the what-ifs or even how he got to where he is. Nope, he keeps moving forward from the first page to the end of the chapter or the end of the book. I could sit here and dissect all the what-ifs and the hows and the whys or I can choose to take this moment as a fresh start, a new chapter or a new book, and keep moving forward!

My Lesson Learned
*Self-evaluation is important; however,
don't allow it to keep you from moving forward.*

My Ever-Present Help
*...Forgetting what is behind and straining toward what is ahead,
I press on toward the goal to win the prize
for which God has called me heavenward in Christ Jesus.
Philippians 3:13-14, NIV*

Lesson #19:

Start Small

My Teachable Moment

It's amazing that at the beginning of every single calendar year I make a long list of "I'm going to do_____ this year." I start off the year excited that my life is going to be different this year! Less than 3 months into it, I begin to feel overwhelmed and eventually feel like a failure by late summer.

I end up getting a boost of "I can do it!" by early fall. That's when we officially start the new school year. I'm pumped, I'm excited and once again a few months go by and I'm back to "I'm such a failure" (of course said with my dramatic voice, hand on my forehead, falling face first onto the bed, kicking, screaming and crying).

Finally, December comes around and I'm feeling all Christmasy and happy. I want to give and give and give! Then, Dec 26 happens...ummmm, our annual bills are approaching and once again I over spent. Back to "failure" position on my bed. But wait...Dec 31! Yes, Lord! A new beginning and this time I won't do the same things I did last year. Here's my new "things I'm going to do" list. Even I have to laugh at this yearly roller coaster ride. I decided that this ride is not one that I want to continue. So, **instead of making my goals so intimidating, I am choosing to start small**.

When our children were newborns, we did not expect them to crawl or walk right away. We didn't stand them up and let go of their hands. Nope, we started small. We nourished them, held them, talked to them and played with them. When they were ready to walk, we held on to them and as they took one step at a time, we began to let go of their hands. Eventually, voila! They're walking and even running!

When I'm teaching our children, I give them the curriculum that suits their age and then each year, I build upon what they have already learned. I do not give a Kindergartner their K – 12th grade work all at one time. Even though our goal is for them to graduate one day, we still start small and build upon it.

Think about these examples when you make your yearly goals (or resolutions). Start small. Instead of buying all your Christmas gifts at one time, start small and buy them throughout the year. Instead of saying you're going to lose 30 pounds, start small and decide to cut out one thing a month and build upon that. Instead of de-cluttering and re-organizing your home in 30 days or less, start small and set 15 minutes aside each night before you go to bed to tackle one section at a time. Then build upon that over the course of the year.

Setting your goals this way, may take you a long time to accomplish them. But, there's more of a chance that you will accomplish your goals and less of a chance that you will give up.

My Lesson Learned
Start small and finish BIG!

My Ever-Present Help
I gave you milk, not solid food, for you were not yet ready for it…
I Corinthians 3:2, NIV

Lesson #20:

Serve!

My Teachable Moment

I absolutely love watching football but I refuse to allow Christian to play (at least under the age of...yeah, never). I love watching basketball championship games only (don't ask because I can't tell you why) but I loathe playing the sport. I enjoy watching soccer matches (even though they are very long with only one real break). But out of all the sports, volleyball and tennis are the only sports that I enjoy watching and pretending that I can play. According to our video game systems, I'm pretty good at it too! But, in reality, I can't play a lick of either one of those sports unless I'm the server.

On the occasion that I get a chance to watch volleyball or tennis, I can't help but focus on the one who serves the ball. The power and the (as my mom would say) UMPH! behind it, is so amazing to me. I even try to replicate that same energy when I play either sport whether it's live or pretend. Pretty hilarious picture, I might add.

While thinking about these two sports, I began getting ready to teach at our co-op. I do enjoy this wonderful co-op and all the support, opportunities, and friendships that have come me and my family's way. However, truth be told, after a nice long break, I wasn't looking forward to adding one more thing back on my To-Do list or schedule. The planning, the cutting, the pasting, the scrambling, the prepping, the researching and more! Of course, the lesson plans rarely go as I planned and all my hard work to prepare the lessons and the crafts end up in a craft that I can barely recognize. My vision is so not the same as a child's vision.

As I'm getting ready for co-op that day, I began to envision the athlete who is about to serve the ball and get the game moving. The effort that they put into serving that ball is the same effort I can put into serving God's children. After all, He has entrusted me with this task in this season of my life. Therefore, I owe Him my all, my UMPH!

When we serve in the arenas that God has us in, whether it's working outside the home or inside the home, in marriage or in an engagement season, in parenthood or ministry, we have to remember that we are serving for God and not necessarily for the person or persons that benefit from you serving (Colossians 3:23-24).

Watching the volleyball and tennis server, I think about the power behind the serve but I also think about whether or not that ball is going over the net. Sometimes, the server puts so much power behind the serve that you are left wondering what happened when the ball didn't make it over the net.

 I like to look at servanthood in this way – when I'm serving for the wrong reason or serving in a capacity that was not meant for me to serve in, no matter what kind of effort I put into it, I will not have the same result as if I did it for God. The ball will not go over the net to really reach the people the way it was intended to reach them.

But, oh what joy the server has when they put all their power into that serve and they are actually able to score on that serve! Man, they hop up and down for joy in the same way I hop up and down for joy when I am able to score on my opponent in a video game!

The joy that I have when I serve God with all my heart and strength and then watch Him carry that "ball" across the net and touch the people He intended to be touched, is so great! Then God takes it a step further and scores on my behalf and not only honors me but blesses me as well (John 12:26 and Hebrews 6:10), Whoa! It's such an awesome experience and feeling.

I must remember to serve God with all that I have and then give it that extra UMPH! If I am focusing on God and the fact that I am serving Him and not a person or persons, I won't keep score or an inventory of what I am doing because the joy to be like Him (Luke 22:27) should be humbling enough. **I have to remember to serve and then watch God carry that "ball" over the net to the people He intended to serve that day.** If they don't receive it the way I think they should, it won't even matter because I have released the "ball" and God is the one who carries it over to those who need it. It's truly out of my hands.

My Lesson Learned
Serve, release the "ball" and leave the scoring up to God!

My Ever-Present Help
God is not unjust; He will not forget your work and the love you have shown him as you have helped his people and continue to help them.
Hebrews 6:10, NIV

Lesson #21:

Walk Away Okay

My Teachable Moment

All of my children love to talk. However, Lillian's conversations tend to intrigue me the most at this point in their lives. Why? Because she is very observant and enjoys talking about what she sees and hears. There have been many times that her stories were so detailed that they were hard to believe. Somehow, someway, all of her stories have been confirmed as true at some point. We now tend to say, "When Lillian says something, you have to believe her even if you don't see it."

So on this particular evening, Lillian comes to me with a story that tickled her so much she giggled her way through the entire thing.

"Mommy, there was a fight between two girls in class today."

Now, I am one of her co-op teachers and I assist for the remainder of the day. Not one time did I see a fight (outside of the usual tugging on the same toy "fight"); but, when Lillian says something, you have to believe her even if you don't see it. Okay, go on.

She continues with her story giggling about this fight.

"…and one girl said that George Washington was better, then the other girl said not uh Babac Bomma (trust me this is not a misspelled word) is the best…"

As she continued with this story, I finally figured out that the fight was between two girls arguing about which president was the best president – George Washington or Barack Obama.

This went on for a good five or ten minutes and she ended the conversation with, "mommy, it was so funny." Now, I do not know if Lillian was giggling over the fact that these two girls were "fighting" over who was the best president or over (I'm assuming) the passion behind their stance or even over the words that she called funny (names and the word "president" for some reason). No matter what her reasoning, this conversation humored her, a lot!

Later on that night, I began to think about why this conversation on one hand was impressive (4 and 5 year olds "discussing" politics) and on the other hand why this conversation was kind of sad to me (4 and 5 year olds "fighting" already over politics). I am pretty sure that neither one of the girls (mine included) truly understood why they thought these two men were the best presidents or even why they were comparing those two. But to think, at such a young age, fighting over politics, was a disheartening thought for me.

After hearing about this situation, it dawned on me that the two girls did seem pretty tensed that day. I remember telling them to be nice to each other and then seeing how they treated each other after I spoke to them. I thought it was odd but figured it was over a toy NOT a presidential debate.

With the new election year upon us, this situation between the two girls becomes more and more real and disappointing. So many friendships and family relationships have been strained because of political debates. Tension increases with each passing day. Tension increases within each major party. Tension increases with each campaign trail and with each presidential debate.

It's okay to feel passionate about your stance. It's even okay to be passionate about your likes and dislikes but it's not okay to walk away from a conversation and feel like your opinion does not matter. **Everyone is entitled to their own opinion and their own beliefs**. I am a firm believer in voicing your opinion and standing by your beliefs. I am also a firm believer in respecting the differences of others as well as being open to different perspectives.

Being open to listening and hearing other perspectives does not mean that you have to change your mind. It doesn't even mean that you have to agree with what is being said or done. But be respectful and walk away like Lillian did (without the giggling) – understanding that two people like two different things. Don't waste "fun time" arguing over whose choice is better. ***Speak your peace in such a way that you both walk away at peace (and possibly even wiser).***

My Lesson Learned
With every conversation, make an effort to walk away okay.

My Ever-Present Help
Make every effort to live in peace with everyone and to be holy, without holiness no one will see the Lord.
Hebrews 12:15, NIV

Lesson #22:

If It Doesn't Fit, Try Again

My Teachable Moment

Wrapping up our Skeletal System Unit with a three part test, I took out the mini-model skeleton. At this point in the test, Christian had to put all the organs and muscles back into the skeleton. Feeling very scientific, I went to put the rib cage back on my model once he had completed his test. To my surprise (and a dropped ego level), it would not fit back onto the skeleton. So, I kept trying. I knew that's where the rib cage belonged.

For the next 5 minutes, I tried to force this part on the model time after time after time. Suddenly, like a light bulb literally shined right on top of my head, I turned the rib cage around. Voila! I couldn't help but laugh at myself.

It reminded me of those toddler wooden puzzles. I absolutely love them but I am ashamed to say that I don't necessarily like to watch toddlers play with them…at least not at first. I sit there for a very long time watching them bang the piece onto the wooden board, missing the mark every time. I sit there and watch them try to put one piece into the space that totally belongs to another piece. It's like the screeching sound you hear on a chalkboard (I'm old school. I still use a chalkboard.). Then, one day it finally happens. I am put out of my misery! My little toddlers have mastered the wooden puzzles and are now ready for the "real" puzzles!

When toddlers master this skill, they love to hear words of affirmation such as, "Yay! You did it!" and "You're such a big girl/boy!" Sometimes, they even look for words of affirmation after they put back each piece. It's the cutest thing.

In this same way, some adults (including myself), need the same thing – words of affirmation. Words that let them know they are doing something right or that they have changed. I admit. I can be very sensitive. Words of affirmation I actually crave at various times in my life. So when words are used in a not so affirming way, I hold onto them like I do a cup of hot coffee on a cold and stressful day! I dissect the words that were said and play them over and over again in my head. It's a very bad habit.

I remember having a very hurtful conversation with someone about me. For days, I struggled with what was said about me. This was not my usual "I'm being too sensitive" struggle. This was different. I was so upset about the conversation because what was being said, No Longer Fit Me! It was just like the rib cage I tried to force on upside down or like the wooden puzzle piece that will not fit in a space that it was not designed to fit in. Those words just did not fit me anymore.

You may not allow yourself to let go of things that have taken place in your past and unfortunately, sometimes others will not allow you to let it go either. You may have truly changed but others may refuse to see that change in you. From this day forward, let them know, let the enemy know, and keep reminding yourself that those things DO NOT FIT YOU ANYMORE.

In one of our Bible classes, we talked about taking off the negative things (words, images, attitudes, behaviors) and putting on Godly things (love, patience, peace, self-control, etc). The same concept applies here. **Take off those negative labels and reminders and put on what God sees in you. You are made in HIS image, so you have to be pretty great, like really awesome!**

When any of my children come to me either whining or demanding something, I usually say "that's not how you talk to me, try again." I have learned to stop accepting everything that is being said to me and about me. Therefore, when unkind words are being said (including the silly un-affirming things I say to and about myself), I will say, "That doesn't fit. Try again." I will choose to listen to the voice of truth, my Heavenly Father. He speaks and corrects while affirming us, all at the same time.

My Lesson Learned

I am worth more than listening to and receiving words that do not fit the person who God has created. Try again!

My Ever-Present Help

God saw all that He had made, and it was very good…
Genesis 1:31, NIV

Lesson #23:

Don't Worry, Smile!

My Teachable Moment

As many married couples may feel, after marriage then comes baby in a baby carriage. Well, that was my story…at least, at first. Our son caught us by surprise and to be honest I wasn't sure if this was a surprise I was ready for. We were just about to celebrate our first year of marriage when I found out we were pregnant. My whole world was about to change and by the time Christian was born, my world changed more than I could have ever imagined. I was home; Home without a job for the very first time since I started working at 16. Fast forward…

"I'm sorry. There is no heartbeat this time." These words devastated me and still bring me to tears every now and then. Our third miscarriage and no one could tell us what was wrong. I wanted so badly to give Christian a sibling. I went into a downward spiral thinking that I failed my son, my husband and myself. I even felt like I must have failed God too.

What was wrong with me? I was such a failure…a complete mess, inside and out. Food became my happy place and staying home became such a comfort for me because I didn't have to face the gazillion women who were either pregnant or have a football team as a family. I didn't have to face the question, "you homeschool? How many children do you have? Really? You don't want anymore?" So many people got punched during that season, of course in my head like they do on TV. Ha!

Then one day, two songs popped into my head. One popular secular song written in the late 1980s, reminded everyone of what to do when you are worried. The other song was a song I heard while watching a Christian movie. It helped me to focus on serving, loving and worshipping God while I waited for His answer to my question – will I ever have any more children?

That day I decided that if God never blessed us with the desire of our hearts, I did not want to live life the way I had been for 5 years. I got up from my bed and began to live. I even went on a water slide, which I swore I would never do since I almost drowned when I was 8. Sure, I could have stood up but in my head I almost drowned. No slides for me! Well, that summer I faced many fears. I stopped worrying and started to live.

Ten months after that epic summer, we found out we were pregnant with Lillian! Yay! My heart still rejoices. I was on bed rest for the majority of my pregnancy and when I said that I rejoiced even on bed rest that would be an understatement. I wasn't the only one rejoicing, either. In the middle of one of our school days (in the bed), Christian, six at the time, walks into my room with a very tight t-shirt on, which he wore when he was at least 3 or 4, and his favorite baby blanket wrapped around his neck like a cape. It was the funniest thing you could have ever seen! For a really reserved kid, this was his way of showing his excitement. Hey, I'll take it!

Today, I get to look at my son, who never lost his faith in God, who taught me how to live even when the answer is "no" or "wait." Today, I get to look at my little miracle that the doctors said may not ever happen again. Today, I get to look at our "prayer overflow" of a blessing baby girl who brings so much joy to us and everyone around her. Today I get to hold on to the three miracles God has allowed us to have. **The process may not have been the package I would have chosen for myself but the gifts that were inside have been simply beautiful!**

Miracles do happen. But if they linger or don't come the way you want them to come, don't worry, smile because God's got it all under control.

My Lesson Learned

*God still loves and cares about you
even when it doesn't look that way.
Your story is not just meant for you...share it!*

My Ever-Present Help

*"For I know the plans I have for you," says the Lord. "They are plans for good and not for disaster, to give you a future and a hope."
Jeremiah 29:11, NLT*

Lesson #24:

No More Plagiarizing

My Teachable Moment

Teaching Christian how to write a research paper has been a very long process. We started off small, a couple of paragraphs, and have worked our way on up to a middle school research paper. Even though it has been a long process, looking at his papers now, I'm glad we experienced the growing pains and did not give up.

I remember his very first research paper. He only had to write two paragraphs about snow. I was so proud of myself that morning. I found a pretty cool website for kids that would get him started on such a fun topic. This was going to be easy.

When Christian handed me his paper and I began to read it, I realized that he really did try to put it into his own words but something just didn't seem right.

I decided to look at the website a little more. The more I read the information, the more I realized that he pretty much repeated what was written on the website. So that day we focused on plagiarizing and how to properly quote someone else's words.

The next morning, during my quiet time, the conversation I had with Christian during our writing time, came back up. What did "plagiarizing" have to do with the scripture I was currently reading? It did not take long for the Lord to remind me of an ongoing lesson in my life. I allow circumstances and words to mold and shape how I feel about myself. I tend to take someone else's words (and actions) and apply it to my life as if the words came from me.

During class, I remember telling Christian that plagiarism is taking someone else's words as if they were your own or as if they belonged to you. I also told him how important it was to always give credit to whom credit is due. If they said it, put quotation marks around what was said and attach their name to it; because, it belongs to them.

"For you created my inmost being; you knit me together in my mother's womb. I praise you because I am fearfully and wonderfully made; your works are wonderful I know that full well" (Psalm 139:13-14, NIV). We may not always feel like we are fearfully and wonderfully made. We may not always feel like we are a wonderful piece of artwork. I know at times I have not felt this way at all, but, as hard as it may be, try to remind yourself that **you are wonderful! You are beautiful! You are good!**

Are you and I perfect? Not at all! However, I was encouraged when this verse came to my mind and I hope it encourages you as well: "Being confident of this, that he who began a GOOD WORK in you will carry it on to completion until the day of Christ Jesus" (Philippians 1:6, NIV). You are a GOOD WORK and yes, at times we can be a "piece of work," however, we are still good in the eyes of God.

The next time you are tempted to take someone else's words as if they belong to you, put quotations marks around it and attach a name to it. There are only two names you can use – God or the enemy (and his name is "Satan" not the actual person's name that may be causing the pain in your heart). So, give credit to whom credit is due and No More Plagiarizing!

My Lesson Learned

You are God's Good Work! Anything said or done that does not line up with His word did not come from God. Add the quotation marks and give it back to the enemy!

My Ever-Present Help

For you created my inmost being; you knit me together in my mother's womb. I praise you because I am fearfully and wonderfully made; your works are wonderful I know that full well.
Psalm 139:13-14, NIV

Lesson #25:

The Mom G.E.N.E.

My Teachable Moment

I needed to take a much needed break and thankfully my friends and family members came to the rescue immediately! Christian slept over a friend's house and both Lillian and Caylin slept over their cousin-friend's (a cousin who is like a bestie) house. They all had an absolute ball which allowed Lawrence and I to enjoy having uninterrupted conversations all night. It was great!

The next day I was so happy to see my children. I couldn't wait to hear about all the fun they had. They were all smiling and we all just seemed very refreshed. Then the reason I needed a break started back up again. The whining, the fighting, the yelling, the screaming, the demands and then finally, my bad attitude turned a refreshed family feeling into a chaotic frustrating night.

I yelled, "Everybody! Go. To. Bed. Now!"

With many tears and several hearts broken, the children went to bed. Once again, I felt terrible and for the rest of the night, I reminded myself that I just do not have the mom gene.

The Mom Gene. They are moms who are so patient and creative. They don't yell and their children are super obedient, happy, and play nicely together. Their house is spotless. They look like they work out like every day all day. Their hair is perfect...even their pull back ponytail is perfect...No Bumps! They cook the perfect homemade dinner using ingredients from their backyard and they make healthy desserts. They blog consistently, work in or outside the home and actually bring in money to go shopping or go to the spa. After all of that, they have an actual bedtime regimen and their children are in the bed before it's dark outside. Then, yes THEN, they put on matching pajamas or pretty nightgowns and bless their husbands!!!! What?!?! Showoffs.

Okay, so maybe that person only exists in my head but that Mom tends to make me feel bad about wanting to take a break from my darling children. That mom tends to make me feel like I'm constantly falling short in the area of wife, mother and woman. That mom tends to make me want to throw in the towel because I. Do. Not. Have. The Mom Gene.

I struggle with this often and I'm sure other moms have felt the same way. So Ladies (and Gentlemen who want to encourage the tired mom), listen to this very carefully. **The Mom G.E.N.E.** is in your DNA! If you do not have children right now and you desire to have children, know that you too have the Mom G.E.N.E. in your DNA and I'm going to prove it to you right now.

G: Giving – You give of your body from the moment you find out you're pregnant. For those who have not experienced pregnancy, don't worry. You still have this in your DNA. Because, from the moment you decide you want children, you begin to move towards that goal. You have all given your time, your money, your body, and your mind.

E: Encouraging - Whether you use encouraging words or not, your lifestyle encourages your children and other kids around you to know what to do and even at times what not to do.

N: Necessary – You are necessary! You are necessary! You are necessary! At times you may not feel needed in the lives of your children, especially to those of you who have adult children, but trust me, you are necessary. You've experienced things and have lived life longer than your children. They need you. They need your experiences. They need your wisdom.

E: Everlasting Assignment – Yes, ma'am. Motherhood is an assignment that will last forever. My mom use to tell us, "Whether you like it or not, God made me your mother and I will be your mother until you leave this earth and even after that. You can't get rid of me even if you try. And if you try and succeed, I will still be your mother." I laugh now because that statement is absolutely hilarious to me! And, it is so true. You have been given this assignment, this title, and whether you or they are here on this earth or not, you/they are still a mom.

Even if you are trying to run from the Mom G.E.N.E. and even if you are the one who feels like you nor your mother have the Mom G.E.N.E., understand that the Mom G.E.N.E. is in you and you can't get rid of it. The Mom G.E.N.E., like your DNA, **is not about what you do but about who you are**.

So, the next time you get down about not being like the next mom, remember that you too have the Mom G.E.N.E. It's just up to you to decide whether you want this assignment to be fun and not as stressful.

My Lesson Learned
*I have been equipped with the Mom G.E.N.E.
by God and for His purpose.
(Giving, Encouraging, Necessary, Everlasting Assignment)*

My Ever-Present Help
*For we are God's handiwork, created in Christ Jesus to do good works, which God prepared in advance for us to do.
Ephesians 2:10, NIV*

Lesson #26:

Listen & Obey (The First Time)

My Teachable Moment

One evening before going to bed, I decided to have a slice of apple pie and a delicious tall cup of Hot Chai Tea Latte. As I went into the living room, determined not to let the chaos of the children distract me from the peaceable moment I was about to have. I grew more and more excited with each step around and over toys that were trying to keep me from having my moment. Finally, I made it to the recliner and the table tray was already there waiting for me. I sat down, placed my pie and tea on the table and breathed a sigh of victory.

Here she comes! Caylin, since she was able to walk, could hear and spot food, or someone about to eat, hundreds of miles away. As she runs (well toddling at that point) over to me, I look at her with a smile and allow her to partake in some of my apple pie. However, I began to realize that the more pie I gave her, the more the table tray moved. Without leaving my peaceable moment, I kindly said to her several times to let go of the tray and stop moving it. Did I move my delicious tall cup of Chai Tea Latte? Nope. Because that would mess up the scenery I had going on in my head.

Well as you've probably guessed, this did not end well. In slow-motion of course, I saw the cup fall towards me and my delicious tall cup of Hot Chai Tea Latte rushed out of the lid of my coffee cup. The tea came out as the "oh-no" music played in my head. I quickly grabbed Caylin and moved her out of the way of the Hot Chai Tea Latte waterfall. As I'm changing my clothes, thankful that my daughter was okay, I am fuming at the same time because 1) Hot anything stings when it lands on you and 2) why won't she listen the first time!!!! And, here comes the lesson:

Months ago, I frantically searched every area of my house searching for my children's...

SOCIAL SECURITY CARDS!!!!!

I couldn't believe this was happening to me. I left my purse opened at a function with kids and for some reason they were playing in my purse before I was able to stop them. Could it still be there? No. It had to be at home or someone stole them. All I could think about was the warning words on the instructions that come with SS cards: "Keep your card in a safe place to prevent loss or theft. DO NOT CARRY THIS CARD WITH YOU." I believe they put the last sentence on the card in all caps just for people like me. You know, those who don't adhere to the first warning.

I carried their cards with me because some form was always asking me for them. I have too many passwords and codes in my head to remember all of that (lol). Anyway, for weeks I kept seeing this warning. Every time I looked into my wallet, I kept telling myself to take them out but I didn't listen. Now, I was frantic and couldn't help but feel awful. My disobedience could possibly affect my children. Someone could steal their identity and it was all my fault.

Thank God, I did find all the cards and I immediately put them in a safe place. However, I can't help but think about this incident often when I'm faced with a choice to listen and obey the first time. Sure, the SS Administration would never know if I carry it around or not, but like we tell our children, we may not know but God knows. So the next time your children don't listen or you do not listen and obey instructions given to you, **stop and think about the effect your disobedience may have on those around you**.

My Lesson Learned
Listen & Obey (The First Time). Your disobedience will affect others.

My Ever-Present Help
For just as through the disobedience of the one man the many were made sinners, so also through the obedience of the one man the many will be made righteous.
Romans 5:19, NIV

Lesson #27:

Turn gloomy Into GROOOVY!

My Teachable Moment

One of the joys of me homeschooling has been the opportunity to share many moments with family members who also homeschool. Field trips are the absolute best when you have loved ones along for the ride. This was definitely the case when we decided to go to an amazing amusement park for Homeschool Day.

We were all ready and set to go have a fabulous fun filled and yes, educational, day. Lunches and snacks were packed and we all piled into their van and headed out on our two hour excursion. Laughter and conversations filled the van for two whole hours. What a great way to start a great day!

Screams filled the van because we finally saw the sign for the amusement park. (I wish I could say it was just the kids screaming with excitement.) We are here! We get ready to get out of the van and someone noticed that it was pretty gloomy outside. Oh well, that's okay. A little gloom can't mess up this long awaited field trip.

We step out of the van only for a few of us to jump right back on in. Cold, dreary and rainy! Not what we had expected. We sat in the van contemplating on whether we should just cut our losses and go back home. By this time, the majority of the children were outside the van still ready and willing to go into the park.

Well, the adults decided to follow the children. We all bundled up with the extra clothes we brought with us, pulled out as many umbrellas as we could find, and ran towards the entrance of the park. I wasn't quite sure how long this field trip was going to last especially since I do not like to be cold and wet. As we waited to go into the park, I grew more and more irritated with the weather conditions. I knew God had a lesson in this one and I was just about to find out what that lesson was going to be.

I stood there and prayed my attitude away. And then it began to pour! We decided to still go into the park and enjoy the day. I continued to pray as we stood in the lines to get onto the rides. All the rides we got on, were soaked! Every seat I sat on had a puddle of dirty cold rain water. Since it was raining, the lines began to shorten and the kids (and the adults) were able to get on some of the rides back to back!

I really do not like being cold and wet but **my original funky attitude was conquered with prayer and perseverance. I was determined to turn this gloomy day into a groovy one!** For the first time in my life, we closed down an amusement park! Seriously! The gates locked behind us and the security guards asked us if we needed a ride back to the car, right before they told us to have a good night. LOL! Now THAT was an awesome field trip!

Life is not always going to bring you the perfect conditions. In fact, sometimes things will just seem downright gloomy. Christian said it best after our field trip was over. He said, "I'm actually thankful that it rained. I think we had a better time because we didn't have to wait in long lines in the hot sun. We were able to get on all the rides and get back on them without having to stand in line." Yes! Something that was so gloomy turned into an oh-so groovy day just with a touch of God showing us the "groovyness" in gloomy conditions. So, as you live life day by day and as you encounter gloomy situations/conditions, remember to try your best to pray, persevere and watch God turn that gloomy into GROOVY!

My Lesson Learned
Pray and watch for God to show you the groovyness in gloomy situations.

My Ever-Present Help
Finally, brothers and sisters, whatever is true, whatever is noble, whatever is right, whatever is pure, whatever is lovely, whatever is admirable – if anything is excellent or praiseworthy – think about such things...And the God of peace will be with you.
Philippians 4:8-9, NIV

Lesson #28:

Know the "Coach's" Voice

My Teachable Moment

Most of my Friday nights or Saturdays are spent watching Christian play soccer. Since Christian started playing soccer, we have been extremely blessed with great coaches (outside of a couple of seasons). However, there was one coach in particular who we not only grew to love him, but grew to love his family as well.

This coach coached our son for 7 seasons and every game I was amazed at the listening skills of these young guys on the field. No matter how loud the parents on the sideline were, the boys did not hesitate when the coach called their name to come off the field or move into another position.

On one particular Saturday, we had a lot of family members with us at the game to support Christian. So the game was louder than usual. The guys played an amazing game and won. After that game, I asked Christian if he heard us yelling his name. He said he heard his name and deep voices but not much else. However, above all of the noise, he said he was able to hear his coach's voice.

Christian's coach was not a yeller at all. He was a very soft spoken man who was able to get the attention of 12 very active young guys, no matter what was going on. Since we had been with this coach for so many seasons, Christian was able to hear his coach's voice and the instructions that he was giving to Christian and the rest of the team. The boys were focused on the job at hand and even though they heard the voices of many others, the coach's voice is the one they listened for and responded to.

The following Monday, I woke up with so much on my mind and not enough energy to move forward with our homeschool day. I just didn't want to do anything. Then, as usual, it hit me. Christian never lost his focus during the game that past Saturday. Even though he was surrounded by distractions, he was still able to hear his coach's voice.

Sometimes distractions come in our lives that seem louder than usual. I use to think it was during those times that I needed to hear God's (my coach's) voice the most. However, I'm seeing things a little differently now. Christian's coach did his teaching during practices. So **the team had to learn how to listen to the coach's voice during practices so that during game time, they could hear that voice above all the other voices**. The guys respected and honored the coach and because they love the game, they want to learn all they can from the coach about soccer and how to master and win the game.

So that homeschool Monday morning, I had to rely on God's word to get me moving in the right direction. I read a scripture that I read years prior to this particular day. The scripture, "We demolish arguments and every pretension that sets itself up against the knowledge of God, AND we take captive every thought to make it obedient to Christ" (2 Corinthians 10:5, NIV), reminded me that I needed to get in the game and use what I learned during my previous quiet times with the Lord (my "practice" times). It was time for me to take captive every thought and be obedient to what God has me to do – homeschool my children.

My Lesson Learned
Get to know your Coach's voice (God's voice) before it's time to put His words into action. Game On!

My Ever-Present Help
My sheep listen to my voice; I know them, and they follow me.
John 10:27, NIV

Lesson #29:

Stand Up (Even If It Means You're Standing Alone)

My Teachable Moment

Lillian is pretty quiet until she sees something that's not right happening to someone else. I think about the many times she saw a child take something from someone she cared about, whether it was a toy or a seat. In her small but very bold voice, she would say, "No, No, that's (insert friend or family member name)'s". I love how she stands up for others. However, I can't help but feel a little bit of anxiety at the same time.

I began my "what-ifs" question session. What if 34 years from now she's just like me? What if she wakes up one morning hating this need to stand up for others? What if she gets mad at me for encouraging her to stand even if it's by herself? What if she's lonely? What if her boldness hurts others? What if she decides the pain she feels just isn't worth standing up for others anymore? What if she decides to follow the crowd instead of standing up for what is right?

In the midst of all of my "what-ifs," a devotional "popped" up in my e-mail (gotta love smartphones). This devotional focused on one of my favorite stories in the Bible with one of my favorite persons in the Bible – Rahab! Long story short, Rahab had heard about God and what He had done for His people. Even though she did not have a personal relationship with God, she still stepped out on faith and Stood Up…alone.

Rahab helped two of God's people and in return she asked for them to spare her life and the life of her family members. The two spies were saved and God protected Rahab and all the family members that remained in her house the day the battle took place. (See Joshua chapter 2 – 6 for the full story.) If God can do that with someone who barely knew Him, what more will He do with someone who knows and loves Him!

What if by my daughter standing for righteousness, she protects others from harm (or more harm)? What if she does end up like me? Feeling like you stood up for what was right; feeling like you stood up to keep someone else from hurting…it's not really a bad thing. Was Rahab scared? Absolutely! Am I scared when I stand up? Absolutely! Will my daughter be scared at times when she stands up for what is right? Absolutely! Will she always get it right? Not at all, just like her mother! But **standing up for righteousness, especially for the sake of others, is not a bad lesson to learn or to teach**.

My Lesson Learned
Keep your mind on God and He will give you the courage to stand up for what is right, even if you're standing alone.
(He'll even work it all out for you!)

My Ever-Present Help
Be strong and courageous. Do not be afraid or terrified because of them, for the Lord your God goes with you; he will never leave you nor forsake you.
Deuteronomy 31:6, NIV

Lesson #30:

The Waterslide

My Teachable Moment

It was a beautiful summer day and we were vacationing at one of our favorite places to go. At the time, we only had Christian and I was fighting depression again after going through our third miscarriage. My faith in Christ was wavering and I did not know how I was going to rebound.

I sat on the edge of the pool talking to my mom, who was vacationing with us, and I remember telling her about everything that was going wrong in my life at that time. It wasn't just about the miscarriages. It was so much more. The pain of everything we were going through was so hard to wrap my mind around.

This was the first time in years that I felt this low. You see, I accepted Christ as my Savior when I was a little girl and I so wanted to live a life that represented Christ. My faith never wavered even after my parents' divorce. I knew God was going to take care of us.

Of course, I did not do everything right. In fact, as a teen, I did a lot of things wrong but my faith in Christ did not waver. It wasn't until I experienced a life changing event in college, that I began to question my faith in God.

I knew who He was but I began to stop trusting Him with my life. At that time, I felt like I tried to live a life for Him but all I kept getting in return was pain. For about a year, my actions reflected how I felt on the inside – lost and hurt.

I remember very clearly the night I chose to run back to God. I knew He was the only one who could fix the hurt I felt. He was the only one who could fill all the voids in my life. I knew I wanted to live a life for Christ again and I refused to be involved with anything or anyone that would get in the way of my relationship with Him. As some would say, I was on FIRE for God!

So, sitting on the edge of that pool and finding myself feeling similar to the way I felt in college, was not only disappointing for me but in my eyes, this was unfixable. I felt like I failed God, my family and myself one too many times.

As I continued to talk to my mom that summer day, I looked over at my husband and my son having a blast on the waterslide at the resort pool. Christian was so young yet so brave. He went down that waterslide like it was nothing. He had no fear. Every now and then, Christian would call over for me to come and try the waterslide.

His joy was contagious but not enough for me to go down that slide. I did not want to forget what I was going through and I really was not in the mood to have fun. My mom even tried to encourage me to go and have fun but nothing helped that day.

Not only was I dealing with my pain, I was also dealing with my past. Waterslides were never my friends. I was a little older than Christian when I went down my first waterslide and almost drowned. Sure, I could have stood up but the water that surrounded me and was now in me, was enough for me to panic. One of my oldest sisters helped me up and got the water out of me. So, waterslides and me do not mix (not even when you mix the waterslide with the cutest little boy in the world). Nope, not going to happen!

Then it happened. Christian walks over to me and says, "Mommy, God has not given us the spirit of fear. Me and Daddy will be there to help you." Ugh! This boy just used the Bible on me. How can I say no to that?

About 5 minutes later, I faced the waterslide. With my son behind me encouraging me and his father in front of me telling me that he would be right there to catch me, I chose to go down this slide and begin a new life. That summer ended up being the best summer of my life. And all it took was a father and a son who were both there for me as I faced some of the greatest challenges in my life.

It's so awesome to know that God loves us enough to speak our language. He used Lawrence and Christian to teach me a lesson that I will never forget.

God reminded me that day that in all of my challenges - past, present and future - ***He will go before me and will always be with me. He loves me*** more than my son and my husband. So if I could trust them with my life, then I most definitely could trust God with my life.

Me going down that slide wasn't pretty at all. I believe I kicked my poor husband out of the way and Christian laughed so hard that it was difficult for him to go down the slide after me. Even though it wasn't pretty, I still went down that waterslide!

My Lesson Learned
No matter what challenges you face, go down that slide into the arms of your Heavenly Father.

My Ever-Present Help
The Lord himself goes before you and will be with you; he will never leave you nor forsake you. Do not be afraid; do not be discouraged.
Deuteronomy 31:8, NIV

Lesson #31:

Back to School

My Teachable Moment

It's that time of year again! Excitement fills the air; yet, at the same time, a feeling of sadness hovers over many. It's the beginning of a new school year! Parents are excited to send their children back to school; yet, a little sadness creeps in as they watch their babies grow up. Children can't wait to be back – new clothes, new and improved school supplies, FRIENDS – yet, even they have a slight sense of sadness within the first week.

Summer has officially ended! No more staying up way past bedtime. No more "free" electronics time. No more mid-day trips to the local amusement park or pool. No more….No more…No more…No more….It's all over! Sounds a bit depressing, right?! With all of the no's, why does it still seem like an exciting time of year? Well, once again, it's the start of a new season, a new school year, new curriculum (Yay!), and a fresh new start!

For about two years, I have written various posts on my blog and for about a year I've been stuck in my own personal summer (and I'm not talking about hot flashes, ladies). During that year, I enjoyed my time away from writing. I enjoyed the freedom of not having to think about what others thought about my blog posts. I enjoyed not having to check and re-check the posts for grammatical errors and spelling mishaps. I even enjoyed not having to carve out the time in my busy schedule to sit down and write. In fact, I enjoyed the time off so much that I even enjoyed the thought of not ever writing again.

So as I prepared for the new school year, I realized how much I really do not want the summer to end. I've had a wonderful summer with lots of new experiences. However, even though the summer was great, I know I have a job to do that will force me out of my summer season quickly.

This job is so not about me. This job is about what God wants to do in the lives that I touch each and every day. My children will suffer if I do not move beyond the summer season. My children will not learn as much if I do not move beyond my summer season. Those who will one day have to interact with my children, will suffer if I do not move beyond my summer season. So, it's back to school I go.

This lesson made me think about the "summer season" I've had with my blog. There are many blogs and books out there that you can read and gain so much from. However, there are so many stories within me that I know I must share. If I do not move beyond my summer season, many lives will not be touched by what God has placed in me. If I do not move beyond my summer season, many people may not learn the lessons that God wants them to learn. Or, they simply may not know how to navigate a similar situation, if I do not move beyond my summer season.

My Lesson Learned
Someone is waiting for you to move out of your "summer season" and make a difference in their life.

My Ever-Present Help
Forget the former things; do not dwell on the past.
See, I am doing a new thing!
Now it springs up; do you not perceive it? I am making a way...
Isaiah 43:18-19, NIV

Lesson #32:

Are you hungry enough?

My Last Teachable Moment (for now)

I can guarantee you that pretty much every day at some point in my day, I will hear the words, "Mommy, I'm hungry." The funny thing about my children is that when they say they are hungry and I offer them something to eat, I may hear, "no thank you. Can I have something else, please?" This may go on for about 2-3 rounds depending upon the child. Lawrence tends to tell me that I give the children too many options and I'm pretty sure at least one of you may be thinking the same thing right now. Yup, you probably are, aren't you? Lol. That's okay. My point in giving them options is 1) I like having options and 2) this is when I can tell how hungry they really are.

I remember one day we were out and about and Christian lets me know that he is very hungry. Now, here's a little background before we start the "awwws." He is old enough to set his alarm, listen to his alarm, get up and make his own breakfast. However, on this day, he decided to sleep until 11 a.m. Christian is my stickler-for-the-schedule kid. If we're scheduled to be somewhere the next day, I let him know way in advance.

So, when I told him that it was time to get up because we had to leave soon, he opted to move at the teen phase pace. You know that pace. The pace that drives you nuts watching because you know everything around you is moving at regular speed but for some reason it's like they're in a Slow. Moving. Bubble.

We get into the car and begin our errands for the day. Since I know Christian did not eat, I made sure that I brought some breakfast cookies just in case he got hungry. When I offered them to my son, his words, and I quote, "I would have to be really hungry in order for me to eat those." Because we have gone through this many times before, Christian already knew what my next response would be…"then, you're not hungry enough."

The funny thing about this story, outside of my son's response, is that earlier that day, I heard the same thing said to me. I woke up earlier than usual, exhausted and thinking about when I could get back in the bed. I knew that I needed to get up and spend some time with God. But the bed felt so good and (whining) I'm still so very tired. I only had 4 hours of sleep. (I was up late playing a game on my phone. Totally my fault, I know.) In the middle of my whining and complaining, the words, "then you're not hungry enough" came to my mind.

I desire to have a closer relationship with the Lord. I desire to spend time in prayer and in His word so that I can see and hear clearly His directions for me for the day. I desire to have alone time in the morning while the children are sleeping. I also desire, no crave, more sleep!

However, when I do not get up and feed my spirit, I end up with, what I am calling, "hunger pains." I end up feeling moody, cranky, rushed all day and just plain old blah. So, that morning, I chose to get out of the bed, to feed my spirit. I decided that I am hungry enough!

Writing this book has been such a desire of mine for so long. However, for years, I do not think I was truly hungry enough to set out the time to write it. On that particular day, I learned that choosing to be hungry enough to do the things I desire to do, and choosing to be hungry enough to learn the lessons that I needed to learn, would allow me to share this special journey with you. So my dear friends, as I end this part of my journey with you, I leave you with two questions: **What are you craving in your life? And, are you hungry enough to do what is needed to "feed" that craving?**

My Lesson Learned

Be hungry enough to satisfy the cravings that God has placed inside of you! *There may be times when you will get tired but do not give up. I didn't!*

My Ever-Present Help

Therefore, since we are surrounded by such a great cloud of witnesses, let us throw off everything that hinders and the sin that so easily entangles. And let us run with perseverance the race marked out for us, fixing our eyes on Jesus, the pioneer and perfecter of faith. For the joy set before him he endured the cross, scorning its shame, and sat down at the right hand of the throne of God. Consider him who endured such opposition from sinners, so that you will not grow weary and lose heart.
Hebrews 12:1-3, NIV

~~~~~

Thank you so much for traveling with me on this journey and "listening" to all of my lessons learned from my homeschool day. I really pray that you were able to learn from the good, the bad and the icky lessons to help you through your day. Don't forget to learn from your unexpected journey and to share your story or stories with others.

Lots of love and prayers from me to you!
Trina

www.ingramcontent.com/pod-product-compliance
Lightning Source LLC
Chambersburg PA
CBHW020902020526
44112CB00052B/1203